WALKING the ROUTEBURN TRACK

PHILIP HOLDEN

Hodder Moa Beckett

By the same author

New Zealand Non-fiction
  Pack and Rifle
  Hunter by Profession
  Backblocks
  The Deer Hunters
  Seasons of a Hunter
  The Hunting Breed
  On Target
  The Wild Pig in New Zealand
  The Golden Years of Hunting in
    New Zealand
  The Golden Years of Fishing in
    New Zealand
  New Zealand: Hunters' Paradise
  Holden on Hunting
  The Deerstalkers
  A Guide to Hunting in New Zealand
  The Hunting Experience
  Hunt South
  Wild Game
  More Holden on Hunting
  Fall Muster
  On the Routeburn Track
  In Search of the Wild Pig
  Station Country
  Always Another Hill
  Wild Boar

  Holden's New Zealand Venison Cookbook
  Station Country II
  Pack and Rifle (1995 edition)
  Great Hunting Yarns
  The Way of a Hunter
  Station Country III
  New Zealand Hunter
  A Backcountry Journey

Young Adult Fiction
  Fawn
  Stag
  White Patch
  Razorback

Children's Fiction
  Lucy's Bear

Children's Non-fiction
  Sheep Station

Australian Non-fiction
  Outdoors in Australia
  Along the Dingo Fence
  Crocodile
  Wild Pig in Australia

Front cover photo: The spectacular Routeburn Flats.
Back cover photo: Trampers on the way to Lake Mackenzie with the Darren Mountains in the background.

ISBN 1–86958–763–4

© 1999 – Original text and photography Philip Holden
The moral rights of the author have been asserted

© 1999 – Design and format Hodder Moa Beckett Publishers Ltd

Published in 1999 by Hodder Moa Beckett Publishers Limited
[a member of the Hodder Headline Group]
4 Whetu Place, Mairangi Bay, Auckland, New Zealand

Designed and produced by Hodder Moa Beckett Publishers Limited

Printed by Everbest Printing, Hong Kong
Film: Microdot, Auckland
Maps by Sue Gerrard

All rights reserved. No part of this publication may be reproduced or transmitted in any form or by any means, electronic or mechanical, including photocopying, recording, or any information storage and retrieval system, without permission in writing from the publisher.

Acknowledgements

I would like to express my appreciation to everyone connected with the company Routeburn Walk Ltd. Particularly, I wish to thank John Davies, Chairman of the Board, for allowing me to stay in the company's splendid mountain lodges (much improved since I first stayed in them in 1990/1991) during the three times I've walked the Routeburn and the one time I've walked the Greenstone Track.

On each of my walks I've very much enjoyed the company of the various guides, and Glenn and Rob, my guides in autumn 1999, were the equal of any of them. Especially rewarding was the company of people from various parts of the world. It was uplifting to see their reactions to the magnificent landscape the Routeburn Track passes through. Things shared are almost always so much better.

Special thanks are due to the helpful staff at the various Department of Conservation offices at Te Anau, Queenstown, and Glenorchy. DOC hut wardens at Lake Mackenzie, Routeburn Falls, and Routeburn Flats were always pleasant and open to questions. Until the next time, then...

Philip Holden, Queenstown, 1999.

Please check services, prices and times are current when planning your trip.

Every effort has been made to ensure that the information provided is accurate and up-to-date at the time of publication. However, the publishers and author cannot accept responsibility for any errors, ommissions or changes in details that may occur. The publishers welcome any new information or comments to include in future editions.

ROUTEBURN TRACK
KILOMETRES
0 1 2 3 4 5
Conical Hill
Harris Saddle shelter
Lake Harris
North Branch
Bridal Veil Creek
Routeburn Gorge
Routeburn shelter
Routeburn River
Routeburn Flats hut (ANP)
Routeburn Falls hut (ANP)
Routeburn Falls lodge
Hollyford
Hollyford Face
Deadman's Track
Emily Peak
HUMBOLDT MOUNTAINS
DARRAN MOUNTAINS
Mt Crosscut
Mt Lyttle
Lake Mackenzie
Mackenzie hut (FNP)
Lake Mackenzie lodge
Dart River
TO QUEENSTOWN
Lake Marian
Mt Christina
Lake Roberts
Earland Falls
Pass
Lake Howden hut (FNP)
Hollyford River
TO MILFORD
Key Summit
Creek
Lake Howden
Divide shelter
Mt Bonpland
Caples River
Lake Fergus
Lake McKellar
Greenstone River
Lake Gunn
TO TE ANAU

QUEENSTOWN REGION
NEW ZEALAND
Queenstown
Dart River
Rees River
ROUTEBURN TRACK
CAPLES TRACK
GREENSTONE TRACK
TO MILFORD
TO TE ANAU
Kinloch
Glenorchy
Queenstown
Frankton
Lake Wakatipu
Kingston
TO TE ANAU
0 5 10 15 20
KILOMETRES

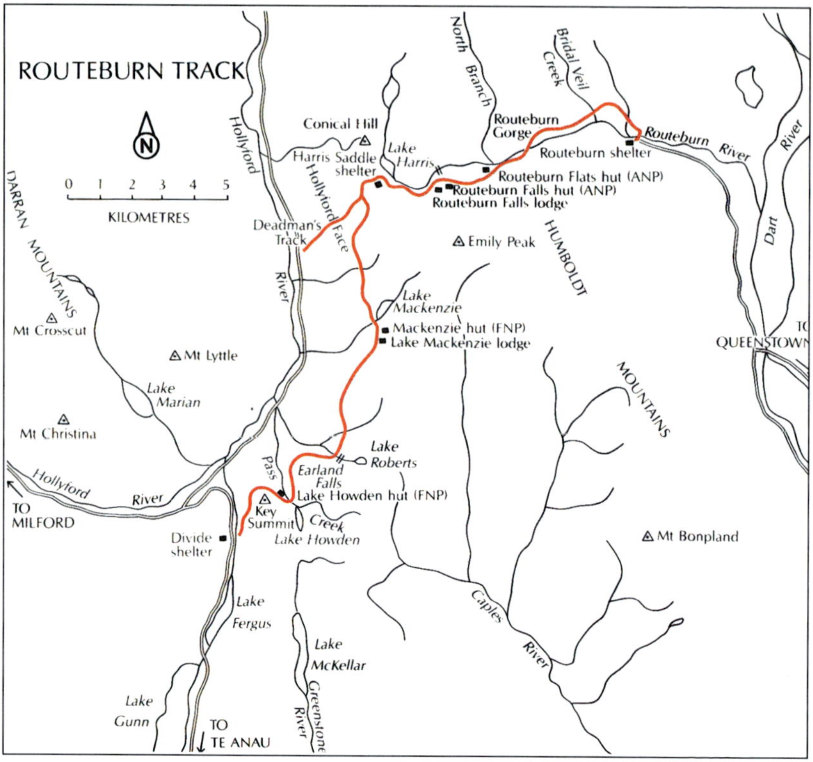

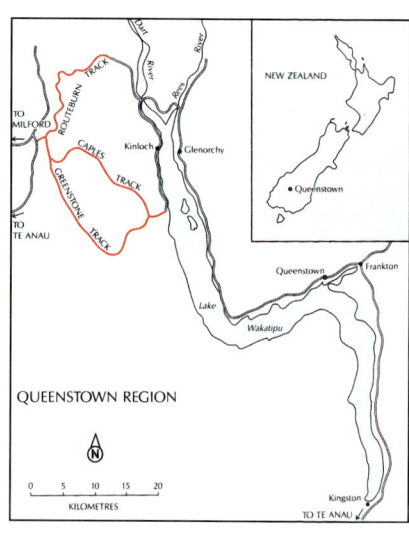

Contents

Introduction	7
Track accommodation	9
Common native birds	10
Animals	11
Fishing	12
Giardia	12
History	15
The Routeburn Track	27
Day One: the Divide to Lake Mackenzie	29
Day Two: Lake Mackenzie to Routeburn Falls	35
Harris Saddle to Conical Hill	47
Day Three: Routeburn Falls to Routeburn Shelter	48
Reflections	53
The Greenstone Track	57
Photographic notes	59
Tramping gear	60
Guided walks	62
Selected reading	64

Introduction

Toitu te whenua
(leave the land undisturbed)

Arguably, the world famous Routeburn Track, which passes through both Fiordland National Park and Mount Aspiring National Park, is New Zealand's premier alpine trek. It offers magnificent scenery, varied birdlife and a stirring history.

Each season around 10,300 trampers (both independent and guided walkers) complete the Routeburn Track.

Most trampers take three days to complete the 39-kilometre walk. The Greenstone and Caples tracks, linked easily with the Routeburn, may be included for an extended walk lasting perhaps six days.

The Routeburn Track can be walked in two directions – from east to west or the other way around. The starting point in the west is the Divide, located within Fiordland National Park, on the Milford Road, 80 kilometres from Te Anau. The starting point for the Mount Aspiring section of the track in the east is the Routeburn Shelter, located 75 kilometres from Queenstown via Glenorchy. Both of these approaches are well serviced out of Queenstown and Te Anau by various bus companies and private tourist operators.

Trampers beginning or ending their walk at the Divide can be dropped off or picked up by Fiordland Travel, Kiwi Discovery, Mount Cook Landline, and Inter City. They all operate between Queenstown and Milford via Te Anau. From Te Anau, transport to the Divide and back is provided by Fiordland Tracknet Transport. The Glenorchy end of the Routeburn Track is catered for by Backpacker Express and Upper Wakatipu Tours, which also provide a service for trampers starting or finishing the Greenstone and Caples tracks from the eastern end.

Any bookings for transport can be made on arrival in Queenstown as seats are guaranteed until 6pm on the evening prior to departure. Also, you will need to have confirmed track reservations with DOC before booking any transport.

Below Routeburn Falls: this is where the two main branches of the Routeburn River converge, with the rapids of the last of the North Branch to the right of the photograph.

Transport options for getting to and from the Routeburn Track

A Depart Queenstown to Routeburn Shelter   8am or 12pm
   Depart Divide to Queenstown   4pm

B Depart Queenstown to Divide   7am
   Depart Routeburn Shelter to Queenstown   10am or 2pm

Note: Please check with the Information and Track Centre that the timetable is current.

Information and Track Centre

PO Box 681, Queenstown, phone (03) 442 9708, fax (03) 442 7038
E-mail, infotrac@queenstown.co.nz

Accommodation, ranging from upmarket hotels to economical youth hostels and backpackers' lodges, is available in Queenstown and Te Anau. There is a holiday park and various types of accommodation in Glenorchy.

The Routeburn is considered a summer walk only. In winter, due to snow, ice, and the constant threat of an avalanche, it is too dangerous for anyone but the most experienced and well-equipped trampers. Even these people would have to approach the walk with the utmost caution. But whatever the season, this is a real alpine trek and one must always be prepared to dress accordingly. In short, the weather is fickle. Never take it for granted or underestimate it – there have been deaths by hypothermia on the Routeburn Track during summer.

Generally speaking, the season starts on 27 October and ends 21 April. The Department of Conservation (DOC) says that advance bookings are advisable. Bookings for the forthcoming season open on 1 July, and for all information concerning this contact:

INTRODUCTION

Great Walks Booking Desk
Department of Conservation
PO Box 29, Te Anau
Phone (03) 249 8514, fax (03) 249 8515
E-mail: greatwalksbooking@doc.govt.nz
Office hours: 9am – 12am and 1pm – 4.30pm (Mon – Fri, May – Nov)
8.30am – 5pm (7 days, Nov – April)

During the season (from 27 October – 21 April), you can also book at:

Department of Conservation Information Centre
37 Shotover Street, Queenstown   8.30am – 5pm

Department of Conservation Visitor Centre
corner Oban and Mull Streets, Glenorchy   8.30am – 4.30pm

Department of Conservation Visitor Centre
Lake Front Drive, Te Anau   8.30am – 5pm

Track accommodation

There are four DOC huts and two campsites on the Routeburn Track. During the season a DOC warden is in residence at each of the huts. They have cooking facilities and gas cookers, communal bunkrooms with mattresses, cold, running water and flush toilets. You may stay a maximum of two nights at each hut and campsite. After the season closes the huts are not staffed, the gas cookers are removed and maintenance work may take place.

Camping is not permitted within 500 metres of the track. There are campsites at Routeburn Flats Hut (30 sites), and at Lake Mackenzie (10 sites).

There is no charge to enter national or forest parks. Trampers on a tight schedule can make short trips – for example from the Divide to Key Summit.

There is, however, a charge to use any of the 600 (approximately) huts under the control of DOC. During the season hut fees on the Routeburn are around $30 per night for an adult and $15 for a child (for booking purposes ages 5–14 are classified as a child). Campsite fees are $9 per night for an adult and $4.50 for a child. All children must be accompanied by an adult. Check the current charges at the Booking Desk listed above.

WALKING THE ROUTEBURN TRACK

Bush robin

Tomtit

Kea

New Zealand falcon

Common native birds

Perhaps as many as 30 different species of birds are found in the Routeburn/Greenstone areas.

In forested regions: bush robin, bellbird, tomtit, rifleman, tui, long-tailed cuckoo, yellow crowned parakeet, grey warbler, silvereye, pied fantail, kaka and morepork.

Rivers, river-flats and lakes: blue duck, paradise duck, pipit and cormorant.

Above the bush line: rock wren, pipit, kea and New Zealand falcon.

Though it's not often seen, the bellbird, with its pure, bell-like song, is the most commonly heard bird in the forest. It has an olive-green plumage and an arched beak. Recognisable by its dark, shiny feathers is the bigger tui. It is a born mimic and, if so inclined, can perfectly imitate many birds, including the bellbird.

Because of its friendly disposition, the bush robin follows trampers along forest trails to feed on invertebrates that may be disturbed. A fantail, seldom still, may delight you with a display of its fan-like tail. New Zealand's smallest species is the palm-sized rifleman, complete with stumpy tail. Somewhat larger than the rifleman is the rock wren which is usually seen above 1200 metres. The pipit may nest in grassy river beds as well as in the tussock field above the bush line.

INTRODUCTION

Animals

Red deer and chamois, occurring in low numbers, are scattered throughout areas of both Fiordland and Mount Aspiring National Parks. A few whitetail deer, extremely wary, inhabit the lower Routeburn Valley. Considerably more plentiful, and quite often seen by trampers, are the fallow deer found in both the Greenstone and Caples valleys.

Hunting in Fiordland National Park is carried out on a block system. Hunting is not permitted within one kilometre of any walking track and, in my considered opinion, should not be allowed in even the same watershed. Refer to DOC, Te Anau, for hunting information.

Hunting in the main valley of the Routeburn is not permitted but is allowed all year in the North Branch. Permits can be obtained from DOC, Glenorchy. However, hunters should note that the North Branch of the Routeburn is well used by trampers and, again in my opinion, they would be well advised to hunt elsewhere.

A hunting season is in force in the Greenstone/Caples area, termed the Wakatipu Recreational Hunting Area. It runs from 1 April to 31 August. As many as seven hunters might be found in each valley at any given time. Hunters also have full use of the huts. In this period, may I suggest that trampers leave their boot marks in another river valley entirely.

Hares occur quite frequently in both the Routeburn and Greenstone valleys. They are mostly observed in the open grasslands and the adjacent, low-lying forest. They also inhabit the upper slopes of the mountains, ranging well above the highest level of the Routeburn Track.

While they may be seen at dusk in the Routeburn Valley, long tailed bats are rare.

From the track I have observed a fine buck chamois below Lake Harris. I have also seen signs of red deer in the Orchard, on the Hollyford Face. At night they feed on the leaves of the ribbonwood which is a favourite deer palatable. For obvious reasons, wildlife tends to give the track a wide berth during daylight hours. However, if you set off early in the morning, you may be pleasantly surprised by what you see.

Fishing

There are rainbow and brown trout in the lower Routeburn (up to the gorge) and in the Greenstone and Caples rivers. Lake Howden contains brown trout but Lake Mackenzie and Lake Harris have only fully protected native trout.

Fishing licences can be obtained from DOC visitor centres, sports shops and 24-hour petrol stations.

Giardia

Giardia is a parasite, invisible to the naked eye, that causes serious stomach illness. There is evidence to suggest that giardia is rampant throughout New Zealand's high country. Take no chances. Kill the cysts by bringing drinking water to a rapid boil for at least three minutes.

With the Darren Mountains in the background, and the Hollyford Valley below them, independent trampers are seen after leaving the Harris Saddle, en route to Lake Mackenzie via the Hollyford Face.

INTRODUCTION

Looking across the flats into the North Branch of the Routeburn, with Mount Somnus on the skyline.

WALKING THE ROUTEBURN TRACK

Lake Mackenzie. The DOC hut nestles near the water's edge, while the track in the nearby clearing passes the Routeburn Walk Ltd accommodation.

History

Pounamu, also called greenstone, nephrite or jade, was as precious to the early Maori settlers as gold was to the European prospectors of later years. Given spiritual qualities, the stone of the gods was used to make tools, weapons and ornaments, and the possession of greenstone meant power. Archeological evidence suggests that by AD 1500 the Maori had found greenstone in what is now called the Routeburn Valley. Maori villages were found on the banks of the Routeburn (Te Komama), and greenstone was discovered below the topsoil.

The lovely region at the head of Lake Wakatipu was known to the Maori as Wai-pounamu, meaning 'greenstone water'. The traditional Maori directions for their well-used trail from Wai-pounamu to the large Maori settlement of Kotuku ('white heron'), now called Martins Bay, still survives. Going up Whakatipua-wai-maori ('freshwater lake created by the demon', Lake Wakatipu) you pass Wawahi-waka ('place where canoes are kept', Tree Island) and follow on up Te Awa whakatipua ('Whakatipua river', Dart River), then enter Te Komama ('running out of a small opening', Routeburn). At the head of the valley cross Ka-mauka-whakatipua ('Whakatipua mountains', Ailsa Mountains) by Tarahaka whakatipua ('Whakatipua Saddle', Harris Saddle). Descend to Whakatipua-kotuku ('Whakatipua to Kotuku', Hollyford River), and follow it down past Wawahi-waka (Lake Alabaster) to Whakatipua-wai-tai ('saltwater Whakatipua', Lake McKerrow). Kotuku was located at the mouth of the McKerrow River.

The last Maori expeditions to the Routeburn in quest of pounamu took place in the 1850s.

In 1855, David and Peter McKellar set sail from Melbourne, Australia, with 300 head of sheep, disembarking at Bluff. The brothers took up land on the Waimea Plains in northern Southland and called their run Longridge station. In 1861, David McKellar and George Gunn, another Southland run holder, headed up the Mararoa River, west of Lake Wakatipu, looking for land suitable for sheep. Eventually they came to the Greenstone valley, via a low pass linking it to the Mararoa. Upstream, they discovered what McKellar described as 'a beautiful lake entirely surrounded by bush, about two and a half miles long by one mile wide... On the banks were patches of a square form overgrown with long grass – evidently the remains of

WALKING THE ROUTEBURN TRACK

Early morning sunlight infiltrates stunted beech forest near Lake Mackenzie.

On Key Summit. Emily Pass, above Lake Mackenzie, can be seen on the skyline between the second and third person on the left.

native gardens.' Naturally, the lake was named after McKellar.

Soon McKellar and Gunn were climbing up through primeval forest. They broke out of the trees and came to stand on Te Tatau-a-Raki (Key Summit), the first Europeans to do so.

Patrick Quirk Caples was lured to Otago by the gold rush of the early 1860s. By 1863 he was panning for gold in the Dart; he found coarse gold in several locations.

One of the main problems facing gold mining interests in this area was its remoteness. The trip to Dunedin was slow and tedious as there were no good roads, yet rumours circulated that there was an easy route to Martins Bay on the West Coast, through the mountains north-west of Lake Wakatipu. In early 1863, Patrick Caples, in his capacity as a member of the Otago Mining Board, packed up and headed west to find out if the route really existed.

The valley he entered was narrow at its mouth but, as he soon discovered, it opened up considerably. In his report to the secretary of the goldfields, Caples called this Western Creek (later renamed Routeburn). In the lower reaches of the river, Caples hid some of his supplies. Eventually he neared the head of the valley, a comparatively flat area of boggy ground. A waterfall cascaded down from what appeared to be an overhanging valley; he climbed towards it. Although it was mid-summer, there was snow on the tops. Following a short but stiff ascent, he reached an ice-locked basin. It contained a small lake, which he named after the Superintendent of Otago, John Hyde Harris. Using his miner's shovel to cut footholds in the ice, Caples skirted the lake, and presently he came to a fog-bound saddle; this too was named after Harris.

Caples records descending 'the steep mountainside covered with timber'. At its base, he reached the banks of a 'rapid-flowing river about the size of the Waipori [near Dunedin]'. This he named after his Irish birthplace, Hollyford. He spent several days searching for gold in the Hollyford, without luck so, running short of food, he re-crossed the Harris Saddle, again under mist, and returned to his cache of supplies in the lower Routeburn.

Caples then backtracked to the saddle. This time the weather was clear. From the saddle, he could see that to the north-west the Hollyford River entered a long and narrow lake before sweeping on to Martins Bay. Caples named the lake after the surveyor James McKerrow.

At the same time in Dunedin, Dr James Hector, Provincial Geologist, was also wondering if a good route to Martins Bay really did exist. He had studied the report compiled by McKellar and Gunn and thought the Greenstone River might hold the answer. In March 1863, he explored the Greenstone to its head, in the company of Von Tunzelman, runholder at Fern Hill station, on the western shores of Lake Wakatipu.

In May, Caples had still not returned, and Hector sailed from Dunedin to Martins Bay. Captain Howell, the ship's master, suggested to Hector that he seek out Henare Paremata, a local Maori who knew the country around Martins Bay well. If anyone knew the old Maori route from Martins Bay to Wakatipu, he would.

Paremata joined Hector's party and in September they set off upriver. Hector named it the Kaduku River, unaware that Caples had already named it the Hollyford. Presently they came to a lake Paremata called Wawahi-waka, but which the Europeans had already discovered and named Lake Alabaster.

Pressing on without their whaling boat, they came to a long and narrow lake, which Hector named Lake Kakapo, unaware that Caples had named it McKerrow. Many miles further on they reached a 'strong creek', surging into the river; today this is called Pass Creek. Henare Paremata directed them up the creek, stating that this was the way to reach the Greenstone. After a hard slog, they reached the top of a 'bald hill' on the west side of the Greenstone valley. Hector was sure this was what McKellar and Gunn had referred to as Key Summit, and he was right. By following the Greenstone, Mararoa and Von river valleys, Hector and his party arrived at last in Queenstown on 4 October 1863.

Hector's arrival in Queenstown had enormous impact. The hero, who had been feared lost, had arrived with the most magnificent news: a practical route to Martins Bay did exist. When Hector rose to speak at a public meeting on the evening of his arrival, he was greeted with prolonged cheering. He told the meeting that a road could be constructed at moderate expense, and the jubilant gold miners were able to visualise bullion-laden coaches, under armed police escort, making the short run to Martins Bay.

Hector soon carried on to Dunedin, anxious to report back to the Provincial Government. The Dunedin newspapers had written glowing accounts of Hector's trip, stating emphatically, 'There will be soon a trade route from Melbourne to Martins Bay and overland to Queenstown and Dunedin'. But the road to the west did not eventuate. Surveyors J.T. Thomson and Francis Howden looked into the matter, and found that Hector's estimate of 'moderate expense' simply did not hold water.

HISTORY

Thomson believed it would cost all of £125,000 to build the road. Moreover, there were many bankers and businessmen in Dunedin who did not want a packhorse track linking Wakatipu and Martins Bay, let alone a road suitable for wagons. A road meant gold bullion from the Queenstown district would end up in Australian rather than Dunedin banks. The Provincial Government, under some pressure, established instead good coaching roads between Dunedin and the western goldfields.

In 1867 James Macandrew became Superintendent of Otago. It was his dream to establish a bustling port at Martins Bay, as closer trading links with Australia could only be good for the province as a whole. In 1868 a select committee was appointed by the Provincial Council to enquire into all aspects of his proposal, and the committee recommended that a settlement be formed at Martins Bay. They noted that 'the entrance from the sea-board to the bay, river and lake is comparatively easy and safe for coastal steamers'; they did not take submissions from the three surveyors who had

The Hollyford River Valley as seen from the Milford Road (below the Divide). The Hollyford Face (Day Two on the Routeburn Track) can be seen above the bushline, extreme left of photograph. Emily Pass is to the right of that.

19

written negative reports as to Martins Bay's suitability for settlement.

The committee decided to attract settlers to the new region by offering free land, and work would commence forthwith on a bridle track between Wakatipu and Martins Bay. Surveyor James McKerrow was called upon to help decide the route, and he rejected Hector's Greenstone route, preferring the Routeburn.

In 1870 Martins Bay was surveyed and two years later the first buildings were erected. The township was, appropriately enough, named Jamestown. Meanwhile, work had started on a bridle track in the lower Routeburn. Macandrew's dreams of making Jamestown a thriving settlement soon foundered. In July 1870 the *Esther Ann*, bringing the first settlers from Dunedin, arrived off Martins Bay in atrocious weather. Captain Thomas Benchley considered it prudent 'to run for the entrance of the river in order to save both life and property'. In pounding surf, the ship approached the Hollyford Bar, a dangerous sandspit. Raging seas broke over her decks and pounded her sides. She slewed sideways, dangerously out of control, and was driven aground and sank. No lives were lost, but almost everything else on board was.

Looking across the Hollyford Face towards Ocean Point. A small bridge (foreground) and the track can be clearly seen.

Late in 1870 the *Tairoa* arrived off the bay, which was great news for the settlers. They were running desperately short of supplies. The *Tairoa* crossed the dangerous sandspit without incident, but she ran aground on her return downriver. It became clear to the settlers that their survival depended on an inland service from Wakatipu. But what chance was there of the road being built? Money from the Provincial Government was tight and work on the bridle track was slow. By December only 20 kilometres had been finished – at that rate it would take years for the road to reach them.

By 1872, without a regular steamship service and with work on the trail slowing, the settlers at Jamestown had been, to all intents and purposes, abandoned. Supplies of food began to run dangerously low; unless something was done quickly they would starve and no one would be any the wiser.

William Henry Homer was by far the most experienced bushman in their midst, so, on 20 September, he set off overland to Queenstown. Upon reaching the Harris Saddle, he found the snow was much deeper than he had anticipated. He stumbled on, often sinking to his thighs. Suddenly the ground gave way beneath him and he found himself at the bottom of a three-metre ice cave. He managed to escape his icy prison but was badly shaken and weak and, faced with the prospect of the same thing happening again, he turned tail. Back in the Hollyford Valley, he continued upriver until he came to Pass Creek and eventually Greenstone Pass, which was not under snow. Finally Homer stumbled into Queenstown, 'a moving bundle of rags, scratches and bruises'.

A steamer was soon dispatched from Nelson with, among other items, 'five tons of flour, five tons of potatoes, one ton of sugar, and fifteen boxes of tea'. Even Macandrew admitted that a mistake had been made in attempting to establish a settlement at Jamestown, but a few hardy souls remained there, to eke out a living of sorts. A packhorse trail from Wakatipu to Martins Bay, via the Greenstone, was put through by the Provincial Government in 1881 – which the five remaining families in Jamestown must have appreciated. By 1883 the town was deserted.

The early 1880s saw the Bryant family of Kinloch, a landing place on the upper north-west shores of Lake Wakatipu, begin their long association with the Routeburn Track. A Cornishman, Richard Cogar Bryant, had joined the New Zealand police force and was posted to Queenstown. In 1870 he purchased land at Kinloch and there he built two homes, one of which became the Glacier Hotel.

WALKING THE ROUTEBURN TRACK

Early morning at Routeburn Falls Hut. A DOC hut warden is about to write the weather report on an information board.

HISTORY

Richard Bryant clearly saw the potential of the nearby Routeburn as a tourist venture. His idea was to bring tourists by launch from Queenstown, with accommodation provided at his hotel, and then conduct horseback treks up the Routeburn using the now overgrown bridle track. The track was reopened and a hut was built on the upper Routeburn Flats, where Routeburn Flats Hut stands today. Richard Bryant supervised operations, and one of his sons, 15-year-old Harry, acted as a guide.

The venture proved so successful that soon other guides were hired and a family friend, Harry Birley of Glenorchy, was invited to become a partner. They continued to run tours throughout the 1880s and 1890s.

In 1912 Thomas Mackenzie, a keen tramper, was appointed Minister of Tourism. The Routeburn Track had fallen into disrepair, but Mackenzie arranged for government funds to be used to reopen it and build a new hut. It occurred to Mackenzie that the walk could be made even more attractive with a new track, mostly above the bushline, between Harris Saddle and Lake Howden. He commissioned Harry Birley to carry out a field survey. Birley discovered a beautiful little lake, which he named after Mackenzie. In his written report, he suggested a practical route.

A year later, in 1913, the Public Works Department swung into action with shovels, picks and wheel barrows. They worked in two gangs, one working from Lake Howden to Lake Mackenzie, and the other from Harris Saddle to Lake Mackenzie. Supplies were brought in by packhorse, and Tom Bryant, Richard's youngest son, was in charge of those operations. It was not without difficulty: extensive bog fields in the upper Routeburn (beyond the present-day Routeburn Falls huts), which had sorely tested trampers and badly frightened horses, had somehow to be overcome. Bryant's solution was to cut large amounts of snow tussock and criss-cross it on the worst of the swampy ground.

Work was completed on the easier Lake Howden to Lake Mackenzie stretch by the winter of 1914. A couple of months later the work on the other section was all but done, but in August word came through to the workers that the British Empire was at war. They downed tools and set off to do their bit for King and Country.

In the aftermath of the First World War there was no hurry to complete that last kilometre. Jim Gilkison recalls that when he walked the track for the first time in 1920 it still hadn't been finished. 'We made good time until we came to the place where work had stopped in 1914, and here we found a great heap of picks, shovels and wheel barrows, where the men had discarded them in their haste to enlist for the war. To our horror there was no more track, so it took us several hours of hard work through virgin bush until we emerged at the end of Lake Mackenzie.'

At the tail-end of the 1920s, yet another Kinloch-based Bryant became involved in the Routeburn. Harry, Tom Bryant's son, ran a motor bus service from Kinloch to the start of the Routeburn Track. These day trips, which began on the TSS *Earnslaw* out of Queenstown, proved so popular that Harry soon bought two more open-air charabancs. With bookings still solid in the late 1930s, he built a small shelter at the start of the Routeburn Track in a clearing near the swing bridge. A few years later he replaced it with a much larger hut, 200 metres downstream.

Until 1930 there had been no road beyond Te Anau. During the Depression years of the 1930s, however, relief workers had built a road up the Eglinton Valley, over the Divide, and on to the start of the Homer Tunnel. The last stretch – Lake Howden to the Divide – was finished in 1939.

In 1953 Harry Bryant commissioned the most famous lodge of all. This large complex was constructed of red beech at the eastern end of the track. It featured landscape windows and a huge, open fireplace. For trampers coming off the track in adverse weather it was a sight for sore eyes. During the peak holiday season, as many as six bus loads of tourists and trampers had lunch at the lodge. Harry's wife, Connie, was kept busy preparing mountains of sandwiches and scones and enormous venison loaves – in the 1950s there were red deer in huge numbers in the Glenorchy district.

With the numbers of freedom walkers increasing each year, the Fiordland Park Board built a 20-bunk hut at Lake Mackenzie in the mid-1960s. A badly smoking fireplace drove trampers to distraction and the hut was replaced in 1978 with a two-storey structure. Also in the mid-1960s a shelter for day use only was erected at Harris Saddle. The site proved too soft and the shelter was later moved to a more rocky site, on the track itself.

In 1968 Jim Gilkison took the plunge and formed Routeburn Walk Ltd. Playing it safe, he made arrangements to use the Park Board huts before building his own. Such was the demand for his guided walk that in the following year Gilkison built huts on Lake Mackenzie and at Routeburn Falls. They had running water, gas or kerosene heaters and, eventually, gas-heated water. Very upmarket for the late 1960s. Following a nasty bout of influenza, Jim Gilkison reckoned that to stay in business he needed a much younger partner. He approached a Dutchman, Antonius 'Ton' Snelder, who had fallen in love with the Routeburn Track.

HISTORY

In 1962 a road had been constructed between Queenstown and Glenorchy, but it was not until 1970 that the *TSS Earnslaw* was withdrawn from the Glenorchy run. The effect on Kinloch was traumatic. With talk of a bridge spanning the Dart River rife in the early 1970s, Harry Bryant could see that his days in the Routeburn tourist industry were numbered. In 1973 he sold his lodge to the Mount Aspiring Park Board. A year later the Dart River was spanned and in 1976 Harry's famous open-air buses stopped running. The lodge stood until February 1981, when the Park Board replaced it with a more modern structure in line with park standards.

Jim Gilkison gradually phased out his activities with Routeburn Walk Ltd. Ton Snelder ran the operation until 1989, when he sold the company to Trojan Holdings, a Queenstown firm spearheaded by John Davies. Wellington born but Dunedin raised, John Davies first came to the Wakatipu district in 1961, where he worked as a high-country musterer. He became a successful businessman, was the Mayor of Queenstown for six years, and is today the sole owner of Routeburn Walk Ltd.

The Dart River Valley, contained by the Humboldt Mountains to the west, above Lake Wakatipu.

The Routeburn Track

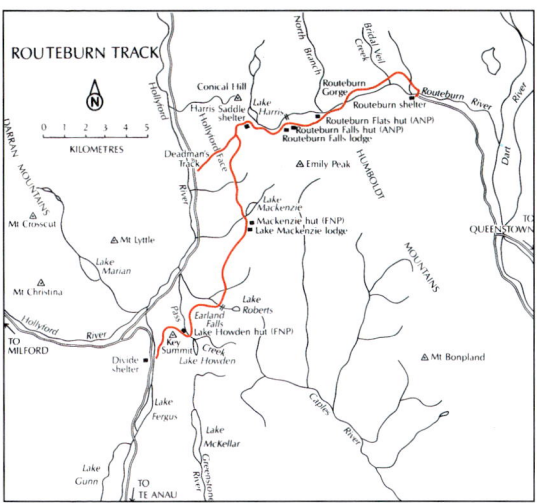

There is, I believe, almost always a wonderful sense of freedom and adventure when you're about to tackle a major walking track such as the Routeburn for the first time. Significantly, the impact does not lessen the second or even third time you cover the same ground. It seems to me that one's overall impression of the track is actually enhanced the more times you do it.

Again there is the weather to take into consideration. I have talked with trampers who have covered the entire track in mist and rain, others who encountered varied weather, sunny one day and raining the next, and some who walked the track in heat-wave conditions as was the case during the summer of 1998–99. No two walks on the Routeburn, due to the unpredictable climate, can ever be quite the same and this is one of the walk's greatest attractions.

Left: After climbing up from Lake Mackenzie, and before continuing along the Hollyford Face, an independent tramper pauses to take a snapshot.

Above: Lake Howden, with the Ailsa mountains (left) rising above the Greenstone River Valley.

Left: following heavy rain, a side creek, not far from the Divide, is running high.

Day One: the Divide to Lake Mackenzie

The Divide separates the Eglington Valley to the east and the upper Hollyford Valley to the west. Situated at an altitude of 532 metres, the Divide is considered the lowest east-west crossing in the Southern Alps.

The track leading from the Divide is wide, well-benched and climbs gradually to the Key Summit turn-off (45 minutes). This region is classified as lower altitude silver beech forest. The dome-shaped silver beech (one of four such species in New Zealand) grows to about 30 metres.

The annual rainfall here exceeds 500 millimetres and vegetation growth is prolific. Various ferns flourish, mosses cling tenaciously to rocks and boulders, and lichens drape branches. It is a forest world and smells accordingly: damp and pungent.

Among other trees, such as the rata, the kotukutuku tree can be observed in this area. It grows to about 14 metres and is easily identified by its peeling, reddish-pink bark which reveals a pale yellowish bark underneath.

The kotukutuku is a member of the fuchsia family (of which there are about 100 species worldwide). What makes the kotukutuku so special is that it is the largest fuchsia in the world.

In late spring and early summer, bellbirds and tuis often feed heavily on the nectar of the red flowers of the kotukutuku, and in the autumn or fall New Zealand pigeons find it hard to resist the tree's black, juicy, elongated berries.

Other birds to look out for before reaching the Key Summit turn-off are bush robins, tomtits, grey warblers, and the rifleman.

Key Summit turn-off (790 metres) is signposted. Leave your pack here. Allow 20-30 minutes to climb to Key Summit itself.

Key Summit (919 metres) is a wonderful spot. An amazing array of plants flourish in the swampy ground: sundews, bladderworts, sedges and orchids. You may also see bog daisies, bog pines and bog forstera. It's a botanical delight. Then there is the magnificent scenery. To the west, beyond a sub-alpine ringed tarn, you can see three distinct peaks in the Earl Mountains: Ngatimamoe, Flat Top, and, highest of all, Pyramid Peak (2292 metres). Closer, beyond the valley of the Hollyford River, are the mighty Darran Mountains. By turning around and looking in the opposite direction you can see the high country above where an unseen Lake Mackenzie is located: the distinct U-shaped saddle (above the lake)

WALKING THE ROUTEBURN TRACK

Luxuriant rainforest growth hems in the track beyond Earland Falls.

THE ROUTEBURN TRACK

is Emily Pass in the Humboldt Mountains.

Many centuries before the first Europeans surmounted this spot, Maori stood here. They knew Key Summit as Te Tatau-a Raki, "the counting of Raki". According to legend, Raki, the all-powerful Sky Father, came back to earth to challenge 10 evil tipua (demons). With herculean effort, Raki defeated each of the demons in turn. Then, exhausted, he rested on Key Summit. Carefully he counted his vanquished foes, and, satisfied that his mission was entirely successful, made preparation to return whence he came. Raki's mighty deed is enshrined in the names of 10 Fiordland mountains. Two of those high places overlook the Greenstone Valley: Tipuakahuru (David Peak) and Tipua-ewitu (Tooth Peak).

On my first descent of Key Summit, I heard an unseen bird call from the nearby forest, 'Kek! Kek! Kek!' The call was that of a New Zealand falcon.

It is an easy 15 minutes down the slope from the Key Summit turn-off to Lake Howden. The lake itself, ringed attractively by beech forest, lies below the north-western end of the Ailsa Mountains. Around the fringes of the lake, you might see a cormorant perched on a mossy limb or a partly submerged tree trunk.

The Howden hut has 28 bunks. Lake Howden, which is where the guided walkers take a lunch break, can be seen as the junction of the Routeburn and Greenstone tracks.

The sandfly problem on the Routeburn Track is never more acute than at Lake Howden. Ample use of insect repellent,

The silver beech is the predominant tree on the western side of the Routeburn Track (Fiordland National Park). The massive trunk on this particular specimen suggests it has stood here in the Hollyford River watershed for many years.

WALKING THE ROUTEBURN TRACK

Early morning – the Routeburn Walk Ltd lodge at Lake Mackenzie.

especially for those people more susceptible than others to insect bites, should be applied before reaching this particular spot.

Time to press on regardless.

From Lake Howden the Routeburn Track climbs steadily, it is often rocky underfoot, and the idea, if all this is somewhat new to you, is to pace yourself.

Again you're likely to see bush robins, tomtits and fantails fluttering about the track. Stand still and one of them might check you out more closely.

Given its western aspect, this is mainly a silver beech forest with its characteristic profusion of growth: ferns, lichens, mosses, and plants such as the green hooded orchid. Other common trees are broadleaf, kamahi and kotukutuku. Occasionally, through window-like gaps in the trees, it is possible to see spectacular views of the Darran Mountains.

The Earland Falls are reached after an hour or so. They are the highlight on this leg of the track. The creek has its beginnings in a higher overhanging basin contained by the Ailsa Mountains. Here, as the track cuts in hard to the almost vertical bluffs, the 80 metre high falls plunge down and spray fills the air. The noise, especially following heavy rain, is awesome. It makes sense to don a waterproof coat and be careful with your camera when crossing Sunny Creek via small bridges. In case of flooding, there is an emergency route located a short distance downstream.

Presently the area known as the Orchard is reached: a ribbonwood-dominated clearing with fern growing thickly under the trees. A small tarn is also here.

Apparently, one of the early track workers, upon observing the scattered ribbonwoods, thought they looked like fruit trees and so named the area the Orchard. The ribbonwood has a light green foliage and can also be identified in summer by its white, almost petal-like flowers.

Prepare for a stiff but short (15 minute) climb after leaving the Orchard, before a (half-hour) very steep descent to the huge basin which contains Lake Mackenzie.

Lake Mackenzie is a lovely stretch of water. On a fine, still evening, the reflections of Emily Peak (1820 metres) in the lake are stunning.

On a late summer's evening, I photographed Emily Pass (above Lake Mackenzie) with a 200 millimetre lens, from the Milford Road, below the Divide.

Looking down on the DOC hut and Routeburn Walk Ltd lodge at Lake Mackenzie. After heavy rains the lake is deeper than usual — normally there is no water directly in front of the DOC hut.

Day Two:
Lake Mackenzie to Routeburn Falls

The impression of being far removed from everything is strong on a fine, clear dawning in the Mackenzie Basin. The sun strikes the tops of the high peaks above the lake and then floods into the basin, not yet reaching the dark face of the silver or mountain beech forest located at the southern end of the lake.

The day's tramp begins by crossing soft, flattish ground before plunging into a place of low-growing trees and boulders. The track soon begins to climb, zigzagging all the way to the treeline.

The forest is now a living green mantle – dense and near impenetrable were it not for the track. Stunted beech trees, their gnarled, crooked limbs decorated with greenish-grey lichen, appear to shoulder into each other as though fighting for the same ground. Heavy undergrowth also seems to be battling for space. Massive rocks and boulders, which the track weaves through, are jumbled together like a child's building blocks scattered at random.

In warm, sunny weather all this feels quite pleasant; there is nothing to fear. On a cool, misty day, however, the atmosphere is entirely different; it might be an alien place – definitely threatening.

Apart from the birds already mentioned, I have seen a grey warbler and heard a kaka on this stretch of the track. At Lake Mackenzie I've seen paradise duck and heard a morepork, the small bush owl, outside the Mackenzie Lodge after dark.

Presently you gain the bushline. Open snow-tussock grasslands seem to welcome you after the feeling of containment the forest induces. There is a great view from here of the two huts, which appear like toys. Can the DOC hut, closer to the lake's edge than the Routeburn Walk Ltd lodge, really accommodate 48 trampers overnight? Lake Mackenzie is revealed, occupying a former glacial valley formed at least 10,000 years ago. At its lower end, it is dammed by a moraine, a mass of assorted debris dumped there by a glacier.

As the track continues around the head of the Mackenzie Basin, the ground becomes hummocky, with huge, slab-like rocks embedded in the ground. Geologists say this is the site of an ancient glacial landslide, perhaps formed at the same time as the base of the lake. It is exciting country.

Above: it is a steep climb from the Lake Mackenzie Basin to above the bushline.

Left: trampers on a bluff-ridden section of the track at they head up to Ocean Point.

Ocean Point, with the Darran Mountains (across the Hollyford River Valley) in the background.

For those who walk the track in late spring or early summer, the Mount Cook lily is a visual treat.

Above: A tarn, a little off the track across the Hollyford Face. This leg of the walk has wonderful views of the mighty Darran Mountains.
Left: Three trampers en route from Ocean Point to the Harris Saddle.

So the place you have now reached is a magnificent, almost park-like landscape featuring herbfields, plants and shrubs. You might be in Mother Nature's own private garden.

Above the bushline the birdlife is different: the tiny rock wren seems to favour the habitat on either side of the tree and scrub line, the high-soaring pipit, a true high country bird, might be heard more often than seen, and the New Zealand falcon, swift as an arrow in flight, is sometimes spotted midair or perched on a rock. The kea is almost always encountered on this day of the walk (if not before). They are curious to a fault, much too trusting and very brave. You can see great intelligence in their brown eyes. The kea is the only mountain parrot in the world and is the embodiment of New Zealand's alpine country.

About 1½ hours after leaving the bottom of the valley, Ocean Point Corner is reached. This is where you leave the Mackenzie Basin behind and enter the watershed of the Hollyford River. Pray for one of Fiordland's fine days because the view from here (1175 metres) is spectacular, and the Darran Mountains an arresting sight. Tutoko, at 2746 metres, is the highest mountain in Fiordland's 1.2 million hectares. It is even possible, beyond the north-western shoulders of that range, to

Time to move on from the Harris Saddle Shelter.

The Harris Saddle Shelter with mist engulfing the Hollyford Valley and about to flood the pass itself.

see where the Hollyford River enters the sea at Martins Bay.

The Hollyford Face is by far the most exposed part of the Routeburn Track and it's often windy. Highlights are the Mount Cook lily and the large mountain daisies which flower from about mid-November through to mid-summer (depending on weather conditions).

Other significant mountains across the Hollyford River are Mount Gunn (2050 metres) and East Peak (2158 metres). The creek that flows between these mountains is called Caples – named after Patrick Caples.

While exploring the Hollyford Valley, Caples lived in dread of encountering hostile Maori. One day, near a beach at Martins Bay, he observed the outline of a roughly built hut. Panic! Taking no chances, he did not light a fire that night. He wrote, 'It is easy for a person to find courage when he has law and assistance at his back, but let him be alone and beyond any assistance, near a camp of savages, and he will find how fleeting courage is.' The irony is that the Maori of Martins Bay were far from hostile and later welcomed the Europeans like long-lost brothers.

It is a two-hour trek across the Hollyford Face, until, by angling up a steep little gully, you reach the A-frame Harris Saddle Shelter. It more or less squats on the border between Fiordland and Mount Aspiring National Parks. Available for anyone's use, it is spartan inside with no bunks and no heating because no camping is allowed here. Rather, it is a shelter from the elements, a place to take a break when the weather is nasty.

I have seen it nasty in the Harris Saddle Basin and I have seen it wonderfully fine. It was here, with the sun streaming down, that I spotted a small, slinky, white-chested animal – a master hunter. It was a stoat. And it moved across a rock near the shelter in a way – all liquid, streamlined grace – that could only be admired.

In the 1880s and 1890s, ferrets, weasels and stoats were introduced into this country to control the huge numbers of destructive rabbits. In the Greenstone Valley, for instance, the rabbits ranged as far as Lake McKellar and devastated the lower grasslands. The introduction of such predators, however, was an ill-advised scheme that would prove a disaster for various species of birds, especially those nesting on the ground. The ferrets, weasels and stoats thrived. Over winter, in a classic case of adaptation, many stoats exchange their dark brown coats for white ones.

Here on the Harris Saddle, sheltered from the prevailing southerly and westerly winds and lying more agreeably to the sun, there is a veritable profusion of growth similar, due to its boggy nature, to that on Key Summit.

WALKING THE ROUTEBURN TRACK

Above: The left branch of the Routeburn flows down from Lake Harris through tundra-like terrain. The North Branch travels through the valley (left) and is contained by the sunlit mountain face. In the far distance is the Mount Earnslaw landmass.

Right: Lake Harris. The DOC hut and Routeburn Walk Ltd accommodation are located just beyond the V-shaped valley (middle left).

THE ROUTEBURN TRACK

Above: Routeburn Flats tent campsite seen from near the Routeburn Falls Hut.
Left: The Routeburn Falls.

WALKING THE ROUTEBURN TRACK

The river below Routeburn Flats.

Harris Saddle to Conical Hill

On a fine day, and providing you have the energy, the 250-metre climb to Conical Hill is recommended. From there you'll see a memorable view: the upper Hollyford Valley, Key Summit, the Darran Mountains, the Tasman Sea, and down the Routeburn Valley to the Dart River country, and the Richardson Mountains in Otago further on. It's well worth the extra effort. Allow an hour or so for the return trip.

Just beyond the Harris Saddle Shelter is the highest point on the track (1310 metres). This bluff overlooks Lake Harris.

At an easy grade the track swings down into the upper valley of the Routeburn. This soon becomes tundra-like terrain and the left branch of the Routeburn is still the size of a creek rather than a river. Wickedly pointed Spaniard grass thrusts above clumps of snow tussocks. This is still the habitat of open country birds: rock wrens, pipits, keas and sometimes a New Zealand falcon.

It takes about 1–1½ hours from the Harris Saddle to reach the accommodation for independent and guided walkers at Routeburn Falls. Before you get there, it is worth making a short detour to Paddy's Point, which offers a commanding vista of the Routeburn Flats, a good 500 metres below. The north branch of the Routeburn can be seen merging with the left branch of the river. The river flats are especially lovely.

Trampers pass Routeburn Flats Hut in single file after spending the night under canvas at a nearby campsite.

Day Three:
Routeburn Falls to Routeburn Shelter

By any reckoning it is an hour's pleasant stroll, rather than a hard tramp, from Routeburn Falls to the river flats. Look for red beech on the northerly facing slopes.

The track finally breaks free from the forest, becomes fringed with fern, and heads up the valley to Routeburn Flats Hut. The river, swift and clear unless it's in flood, is off to your right.

Though it wasn't always the case, red deer are not often seen here by trampers. In the early 1950s Richie Bryant came here with his father Harry and Uncle Dick on a spring hunting trip. They arrived at the lower end of the flats in the late afternoon, when the deer, largely undisturbed then, were out feeding. They counted 127 red deer. The grass on the flats was cropped low, the new growth snipped off at ground level. The interior of the adjacent forest was far less dense than it is now. The venison boom of the mid-to-late 1960s and 1970s, when helicopters were used to devastating advantage, saw the Routeburn deer almost totally eliminated.

From Routeburn Flats Hut you look directly into the inviting mouth of the North Branch. DOC says this is an attractive walk, passing through forest glades, open grass and herb fields. There are fine views of Somnus (named after the Greek goddess of sleep), North Col and Nereus Peak. The views from North Col, right out to Martins Bay, are wonderful and you need a full day to enjoy them. There are several bivouacs under huge, overhanging boulders where you can spend the night.

It was at these rock bivvies that a party of prospectors, including Alphonse Barrington, made camp in December 1863. All told there were three men and one dog. Their objective was to find gold in the unexplored mountains north of the Barrier Range, near the border between Otago and Fiordland. The country they eventually came to was awesome – a daunting confusion of treacherous ravines, razor-backed ridges and broken-backed glaciers. It was a scene set perfectly for an accident. Barrington wrote, 'Simonin was behind me; I heard him sing out "Look out"; I turned round and he was coming down the snow at a fearful rate, head first, on his back.' Simonin ended up badly shaken but unhurt, at the bottom of a gully. The third man, Farrell, was in dire straits when a flax rope snapped and he plunged headlong into a frightening waterfall but somehow managed to survive by grasping hold of a rock.

The party failed to find gold in profitable quantities, and, with winter fast approaching, they decided to take a direct route back to Lake Wakatipu. They were in no fit state for such an arduous undertaking; five or six months had gone by since they departed Queenstown and they had faced shocking privation and nearly starved to death (the dog's life must at times have been in danger). Nevertheless, they set off along the tops of the mountains.

Finally they arrived in Queenstown. They resembled living skeletons and 'their cheek bones and noses, besides their elbows, hips and other parts… were protruding through the skin in places.' They were given money by sympathetic miners, and, at a public meeting, praised for their exploratory work.

It is worth noting that the kaka, a forest-dwelling relative of the kea, has been known to nest in the vicinity of Routeburn Flats Hut. Often paradise ducks can be observed on the boggy grasslands.

The last leg of the walk – on the west-to-east crossing of the Harris Saddle – begins here. It is an easy two hours out to the Routeburn Shelter.

Beyond the open river flats, a suspension bridge provides access to the left side of the river. Beyond here, a deep gorge has been formed by the river, which, in the 15,000 years since the glaciers retreated, has displayed its awe-inspiring power by slicing deep into the sandstone.

The track naturally follows the gorge. From certain points, where it is possible to peer down, you may pause to do so, though it doesn't appear inviting because very little sun penetrates the fearful chasm. Massive boulders, some the size of a small house, rear up out of the foamy, surging water as though making a vain attempt to escape; the river thunders, a powerful, vibrant force created in the high watershed of the Harris Saddle when the landmass was first taking shape.

The track climbs high at this point before dropping down to Bridal Veil stream which is crossed by a short bridge. All of the side creeks along this stretch are crossed in this manner, so even in times of flooding access is not curtailed.

Presently the track begins to widen and flatten out; obviously a great deal of work has been carried out on it at some stage. This is all that remains of the 1870s bridle track that never reached anywhere near Martins Bay.

Soon the river comes into sight. Now, having broken free of the gorge, it sweeps on to the Dart River Valley. The Routeburn Shelter comes into view on the far side of the river. A swing bridge, 200 metres further on, takes you to the other side. It is already a time for reflection.

Distances and Travelling Times

Travelling times are generous and allow for photography stops and rest breaks. Figures in brackets give times if walking the track east-to-west.

The Divide to Lake Howden
Distance 3km   Time $1\frac{1}{2}$ hours (1 hour)

Lake Howden to Lake Mackenzie
Distance 10km   Time $3\frac{1}{2}$ hours (3 hours)

Lake Mackenzie to Harris Saddle
Distance 10km   Time $3\frac{1}{2}$ hours (3 hours)

Harris Saddle to Routeburn Falls
Distance 5km   Time $1\frac{1}{2}$ hours (2 hours)

Routeburn Falls to Routeburn Flats
Distance 3km   Time 1 hour ($1\frac{1}{2}$ hours)

Routeburn Flats to Routeburn Shelter
Distance 8km   Time 2 hours ($2\frac{1}{2}$ hours)

Right: End of the track: the Routeburn Shelter.

Reflections
Easter Sunday
At Routeburn Shelter

With much relief I dumped my too heavy Fairydown pack on the ground. With considerably more care I placed my camera gear out of harm's way. Stretching my aching shoulders, I said 'G'day' to a couple of independent trampers who had arrived there ahead of me. They were sprawled out, enjoying the glorious April sunshine. It was one-thirty; all going to plan, the Queenstown-bound bus would turn up in half an hour.

This was the third time I'd walked the Routeburn Track. On each occasion I'd experienced at trail's end a powerful sense of accomplishment. A really good feeling. It also meant that I had now completed the track in three different seasons – spring, summer and autumn. Winter? No, I have no intentions whatsoever of undertaking the track then. Only recently I learned there are an estimated 32 known avalanche paths that cross the track between Earland Falls and the Routeburn Falls, and the implications of that, when snow blankets the tops, is warning enough.

As I mentioned earlier, no two crossings of the Routeburn Track are ever quite the same. And so it proved to be on this, my latest venture. In the past I've climbed to the top of Key Summit in good weather, but this time, because of mist and rain, the effort of doing so wasn't worthwhile. I have gazed at Lake Howden in wonderful conditions and when it resembled a loch in the misty Scottish Highlands. I have traversed the spectacular Hollyford Face in rain and mist (in spring), in dazzling sunshine (in late summer), and this time, in mostly good conditions. On both of my previous trips the weather – between Routeburn Falls and the Routeburn Shelter – was indifferent. This time it could not have been better – warm, sunny and still. Swings and roundabouts, then.

But every day on the Routeburn Track is worthwhile. I caught up with the Earland Falls in full throttle on Good Friday. I've never seen them like that before, what a magnificent sight they made. The noise was deafening.

The Earland Falls, Good Friday.

Later, I reached the Orchard. I had not seen it at its best in 1990 and 1991. Same thing eight years later. Even so, it was still a particularly attractive spot with deep ferns under the ribbonwood trees, toi toi scattered about, and a nice little tarn below on a bench-like stretch of ground. Maybe I'd have to walk the track another time to see the Orchard in a good photographic light.

The DOC hut warden at Lake Mackenzie would tell me that red stags had been heard roaring from the Hollyford Face, down below the Orchard, recently. There's a whole heap of country down there that's hardly been touched by hunters.

As for Lake Mackenzie, well, it was much deeper than I'd seen it before – in flood, you could say. To allow for that there is a detour.

Up on the Hollyford Face, arguably the highlight of the walk, there was hardly any wind at all. Which was heaps better than damn near being blown off the place!

Since I was last there, the shelter at the Harris Saddle had been shifted to another location nearby. Because of the amount of foot traffic the previous site had to cope with, it had become much too fragile. Fragile is a popular word in DOC circles. The Harris Shelter is a popular place for all trampers to take a break, get out of the elements, have a bite to eat and a hot drink. Perched between the two national parks in question, it takes all that the weather can hurl at it head on. On Easter Saturday it was quite cold at the shelter, with either a weak sun on display or swirling mist which took over completely. Though Lake Harris, just over an exposed ridge but in another watershed entirely, was gleaming in bright sunshine and the temperature would have been much warmer. The difference between the west and east side of these mountains has always been great. Even so, the mist seemed to be pursuing me and it covered Lake Harris before I had finished my photography.

The tramp down from this point to Routeburn Falls, where the DOC accommodation and the Falls Lodge are close together, was a bone-jarring affair. Or perhaps I was feeling the effects of it more than I had before? Either way, I was mighty happy to reach my destination that day.

Between Routeburn Falls and Routeburn Flats I'd come to a huge slip – a major landslide. A signpost at each end said it had been caused in January 1994. It happened at night, following torrential rain. The chilling sound it made was heard down below at the DOC hut (Routeburn Flats), and by those trampers under canvas at the nearby tent-site. What on earth was that? That was Mother Nature scarring the landscape. In fact, the rain was so heavy and so prolonged prior to the landslide that whole sections of the track were obliterated. As a result, DOC closed the track at this point for about six to eight weeks. The 'guided' walk carried on, with trampers being flown out from the helicopter pad at Routeburn Falls on the last day of the walk. This option was also open to independent trampers if they wanted it. The alternative meant walking from the Divide to Routeburn Falls and back again.

Meanwhile (with DOC footing the bill) the Army moved in to repair the damage. They built a number of excellent bridges and greatly improved the track. The track has not been closed here since then.

At Sugarloaf Creek, with the walk nearing a close, I paused on the bridge that spans it and took a long and careful look about me because, six weeks previously, a group of guided walkers had seen a whitetail doe feeding quietly on the bank of the creek. That doe was somewhere else today.

Back at the Routeburn Shelter

More trampers had arrived. I grinned at Lawrence – a tall, powerfully built, Hong Kong-based North American. He was soon enthusing about the last three days with Rob, one of the guides. Lawrence reckoned he'd enjoyed it so much he could start it all over again tomorrow. I had no doubt at all that he could have. Me? Hey, I'd need a few days taking it really easy before I'd feel up to tackling it again. The Routeburn Track is not that easy!

The lovely Greenstone River.

The Greenstone Track
(as linked with the Routeburn Track)

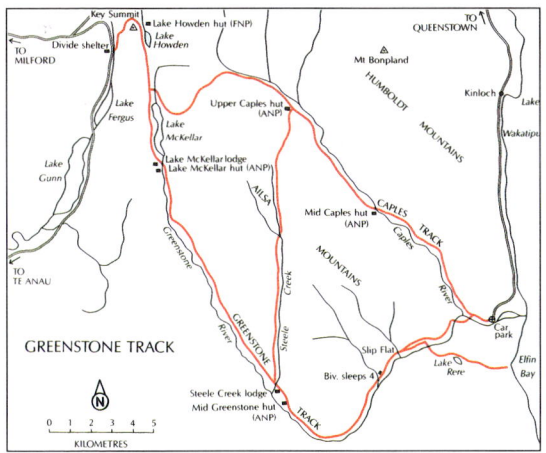

The Greenstone Track begins at the end of the Greenstone Road, 86 kilometres from Queenstown via Glenorchy. Recently, the Queenstown Glenorchy Road was fully sealed and the views of Lake Wakatipu and the mountains on the western side of it, and at the head of the lake, are as memorable as anything you'll see on the Te Anau-Divide leg on the Milford Road.

The Greenstone has been established as a track since 1881, when it created a tenuous link with an already dying Jamestown. When the track was opened up, Alice Mackenzie, a teenager living at Martins Bay, described it:

> '... the authorities cut through the dense forest a rough track suitable for a horse to be taken over. Even so, that did not mean a track where one could ride all the way, for vines and branches hung down to catch the rider and drag him off his horse. I know, for I have been swept off a horse and deposited in the mud at his heels. Trees often fell across the track, and either they had to be cut through or a track had to be made round them to let the horse past. After heavy rain the banks of the creeks would be too steep for a horse, and cuttings had to be made on both sides to let a horse in and out of the creeks and rivers.'¹

¹from J. H. Jones, *Martins Bay*, National Parks Centennial Publications, 1987.

The Greenstone River, flowing between the Ailsa Mountains and, on its right, the Livingstone and Thompson Mountains (beyond Pass Burn on the Lake Mavora walkway), enters Lake Wakatipu three kilometres north of Elfin Bay.

Essentially, the Greenstone can be considered a low-altitude track which follows a wide, open valley hemmed in by the predominant beech forest. The areas of red tussock, especially in the mid to upper valley, are not found on the higher altitude Routeburn Track.

DOC huts: Mid-Greenstone (12 bunks), and Lake McKellar (20 bunks). A lone DOC warden is here in the season, moving between huts as far afield as the Lake Howden Hut. The Greenstone huts are heated only with coal. Trampers must carry their own gas cookers. Camping is permitted along the bush edge but not on the river flats. There is a campsite (10 sites) 20 minutes below the Lake Howden Hut.

The lodges on the 'Grand Traverse' guided walk are at Steele Creek and Lake McKellar.

Note: it is an easy two hours' walk from Lake McKellar to Lake Howden Hut. The low-lying Greenstone Saddle (776 metres) is crossed in this stretch of the track.

Trampers normally leave their packs at Lake Howden Hut and make the detour to Key Summit (too good to miss out on) before pressing on to Lake Mackenzie.

Distances and Travelling Times

Travelling times are generous and allow for photography and rest breaks.

Greenstone Car Park to Mid Greenstone Hut/Steele Creek Lodge
Distance 18km   Time   5 – 7 hours

Mid Greenstone Hut/Steele Creek Lodge to Lake McKellar Hut/Lodge
Distance 14km   Time 4 – 5 hours

Lake McKellar Hut/Lodge to Lake Mackenzie Hut/Lodge
Distance 16km   Time 5 – 6 hours

Photographic notes

Mist moves in on Lake Harris.

Because there is a huge interest in photography today, I've included information on the equipment I used on the Routeburn Track.

I always carried two Nikon F-300 camera bodies (a model no longer manufactured). A variety of Nikkor lenses were used and they include a 24-mm, 35-mm, 35-70-mm, and a 200-mm. Most of the shots in this book were taken with the 35-70-mm and the 200-mm lens. A Slik U-8000 was used without exception. The bird photographs were taken with a 300-mm lens in different locations.

With few exceptions, I used Fujichrome 100 ASA Provia film.

Tramping Gear

Recommended gear for independent trampers using DOC accommodation

Pack everything in four or five large plastic bags, then put these in one large, heavy-duty bag inside your pack. This way, even in heavy rain, you'll arrive in camp with everything dry.

Essentials

Frame pack
Make sure it is comfortable and roomy.
Heavy-duty plastic bag to act as waterproof lining
Sleeping bag
Down-filled preferably.

Sleeping mat/groundsheet/ sheet of polythene
Nylon tent
You may have to camp if the huts are full. A 7 feet by 5 feet tent is about right for two people.

Clothing

Underwear
Socks
Wear one pair of thick woollen socks over a cotton pair if possible. Carry three spare pairs.
Long johns/skivvy
Either wool or polypropylene. The latter has the advantage of drying remarkably quickly. I wear the full set on the track if it's cold. In camp, I like to wear a superfine woollen vest that doesn't irritate the skin.
Shorts
Long trousers
Tracksuit bottoms are good to walk in and fine in camp. Even more comfortable around camp are fibrepile trousers.
Woollen hat and peaked cap

Woollen bush-shirt
The old hunter's standby. You might prefer a woollen pullover or fibrepile garments.
Parka
Overtrousers
Too hot and restricting for many trampers, but ideal in really nasty conditions.
Boots
Don't spare the expense here.
Gaiters
Optional but great in snow, ice, or rough, scrubby country.
Sneakers
Neat in camp and very useful if your boots are causing trouble. Not suggested for use on the track, however, since the risk of a twisted ankle is far greater.

TRAMPING GEAR

Also
Toiletries
First-aid kit
Small torch
Map
  Trackmap Routeburn & Greenstone, Infomap 335-02. A compass is not required on either the Routeburn or the Greenstone, unless you intend getting well off the track.

Camera
  Check batteries before leaving. Take plenty of film.
Sunglasses, suntan lotion, lip protection and insect repellent
  Are all essential.
Cards
Paperback novel
Writing materials

Cooking utensils
Alpine cooker with fuel
2 billies
Frypan
Plastic plate and mug; knife, fork and spoon set

Small folding knife
  Carried in a pouch on your belt or in a shirt pocket. A steel will assist in keeping the knife sharp.
Matches

Food
Since you'll use up plenty of calories, and because the mountain air stimulates one's appetite, nourishing, high energy food is essential. So, with the accent on the weight factor, go for pasta, rice, oats, muesli, dehydrated vegetables and some of the wide range of precooked meals ideal for backpackers. For snacks and emergency rations, take chocolate, raisins, muesli bars, nuts, or a combination of these, called scroggin. Remember to drink plenty of fluid.

Tramping equipment hire
Practically everything you need can be hired at a reasonable cost at the following outlets:

In Queenstown:
Kiwi Discovery, 37 Camp Street   Phone (03) 442 7340 Fax (03) 442 7341
Mountain Works, 27 Shotover Street   Phone/Fax (03) 442 7329
Outside Sports, Top of the Mall   Phone (03) 442 8883 Fax (03) 442 6406
Alpine Sports, 28 Shotover Street   Phone/Fax (03) 442 7099

At Te Anau:
Bev's Tramping Gear Hire
16 Homer Street   Phone/Fax (03) 249 7389

As a working guide to hire costs, backpacks, cookers and sleeping bags are approximately $5 a day, and tents are approximately $15 a day.

Trampers on the guided walk prepare to leave the Routeburn Falls Lodge.

Guided walks

'The Routeburn and Greenstone are two of the most superb walking areas in the world. Dense rainforest with excellent tracks, sparkling lakes, mighty peaks and remote passes supply a sense of challenge without too great a feeling of danger. Well-equipped and comfortable lodges guarantee a good night's rest and experienced guides ensure a safe journey. These walks are an experience that anyone will always remember.'

– Sir Edmund Hillary

An alternative to walking the track independently is provided by Queenstown-based Routeburn Walk Ltd. They operate a three-day guided walk of the Routeburn and Greenstone tracks. They also offer the 'Grand Traverse' – a six-day trek which includes both tracks. The shorter Routeburn walk, however, is by far the more popular of the two options.

This is a package deal which includes transport to and from the track (the guided walk always travels west to east). Accommodation on the track consists of two first-class mountain lodges (with a resident manager in each) which feature hot showers, a drying room, excellent meals, and communal bedrooms. On the final day a group photograph is taken at Glenorchy, and later a celebration dinner is held at a leading Queenstown hotel. It is a particularly lovely way to end what is a truly

GUIDED WALKS

wonderful experience. If required, the following equipment is supplied: a 20-litre daypack, waterproof parka and hood, waterproof over trousers, sleeping sheet, pillow slip and towel. They recommend that you bring:

2 sets of underwear	handkerchiefs (not tissues)
2 shirts	warm casual clothing for evening
trousers or sweatpants	boots or strong walking shoes
shorts	toiletries
3 pairs woollen socks	insect repellent
woollen sweater or thermal wear	sunscreen
swimsuit	camera
warm hat and sun hat	no electric razors

You should put these in plastic bags to keep them dry. Keep your pack as light as possible – this will enhance your experience.

Departure Times

All tracks are open from November to the end of April

Routeburn Walk
3 Days/2 Nights
Departures:
Every Tuesday,
Wednesday, Friday
Saturday and Sunday

Grand Traverse
6 Days/5 Nights
Departures:
Monday and
Friday

Greenstone
3 Days/2 Nights
Departures:
By request with a
minimum of
4 people

For further information contact Routeburn Walk Ltd, PO Box 568, Queenstown, New Zealand

Phone:	In New Zealand	(03) 442 8200
	Outside New Zealand	64 3 442 8200
Fax:	In New Zealand	(03) 442 6072
	Outside New Zealand	64 3 442 6072
Email:	routeburn@xtra.co.nz	
Internet:	http://nz.com/southis/routeburn	

Selected reading: books

Many of these publications are out of print but are available at libraries; others can be picked up at bookshops, tourist offices and DOC centres.

Back Country Huts, Department of Conservation, 1989.
Brailsford, B. *Greenstone Trails*, A.H. & A.W. Reed, Wellington, 1984.
Brailsford, B., & Mitchell, D. *The Greenstone/Caples: A Track Guide*, Whitcoulls, Christchurch, 1976.
Burton, R., & Atkinson, M. *A Tramper's Guide to New Zealand*, Reed Methuen, Auckland, 1987.
Complete Book of New Zealand Birds, Reader's Digest, Sydney / Reed Methuen, Auckland, 1985.
Gilkison, R. J. *Early Days in Central Otago*, Whitcombe & Tombs, Christchurch, 1958.
Jones, I.H. *Early Fiordland*, A.H. & A.W. Reed, Wellington, 1968.
Jones, J.H. *Martins Bay*, National Parks Centennial Publication, 1987.
McKenzie, D. *Road to Routeburn*, John McIndoe, Dunedin, 1973.
Miller, F.W.G. *Golden Days of Lake County*, Whitcombe & Tombs, Christchurch, 1958.
Mountains of Water: The Story of Fiordland National Park, Department of Lands & Survey, Fiordland National Park, 1986.
Salmon, J.T. *Field Guide to the Alpine Plants of New Zealand*, A.H. & A.W. Reed, Wellington, 1968.
Salmon, J.T. *The Native Trees of New Zealand*, Reed Methuen, Auckland, 1980.
Temple, Philip. *BP Guide to the Routeburn Track*, Pacific, Auckland, 1988.
Wild New Zealand, Reader's Digest, Sydney, 1981.
Wises New Zealand Guide, Wises Publications, Auckland, 1987.

Brochures/booklets/maps

Greenstone and Caples Tracks, Department of Conservation, 1998.
Guide to the Routeburn Track, New Zealand Geological Survey, DSIR, 1988.
The Routeburn Track (field notes), Craig Potton Publishing, 1998.
The Routeburn Track, Department of Conservation, 1998.
Routeburn Track Notes, Routeburn Walk Ltd.
Routeburn Walk Or Grand Traverse, Routeburn Walk Ltd.
Routeburn & Greenstone Infomap, DOSLI.